Prisoner Family Talks, Days, Stays & Vacations

Connecting Helps Healing

Reverend Mike Wanner

Table of Contents

Introduction

This Book expands the importance of family to rehabilitation. The potential of prisoners to once again reclaim a bit of the joy that they may have missed. Prison may have suppressed the joy that once was and the separation can leave a person feeling hopeless but reversing the process may be key to healing.

Restoring the family can bring a whole new dynamic to the motivation of a prisoner. This book will be about furthering the healing in families to help all of them heal. To get to this point, the following books were written to build a foundation of possibility:

1. *Angel Raphael Speaks Volume 4: Angels, Addicts, Alcoholics & Prisoners – Oh Yeah!*
2. *Angel Raphael Speaks Volume 5:* Prisoners Caring for Alcoholics - Australia In Miniature Projects Intro
3. *Angel Raphael Speaks Volume 6:* Prisoners Caring for Addicts - Australia In Miniature For Addicts
4. *Prison Jobs Now: Providing Care For Addicts And   Alcoholics*
5. *Angel Raphael Speaks - Prisons* (A Kindle only book -2013)
6. *Contained Care Communities Concept*
7. *Australia In Miniature*
8. *Prison Possibilities Dialogue Series: Concept*
9. *Prison Possibilities Dialogue Series: Volume 2 Dialogues*
10. *Prison Possibilities Dialogue Series: Volume 3 Dialogues*
11. *Prison Possibilities Dialogue Series: Volume 4 Dialogues*
12. *Prison Possibilities Dialogue Series: Volume 5 Dialogues*
13. *Prison Possibilities Voluntary Exile: Concept*
14. *Prison Possibilities Correction Coaches: Concept*
15. *Prison Possibilities for Mexicans: Is A Boat Better than A Wall?*
16. *Prison Possibilities Family Time:* A Reason to Thrive!
17. Prison Genius Pool: *"So Much Genius In Jail"*
18. *Prison Possibilities Access Systems: Prisoner Access by Request*
19. *Prisoner's Lawyers Can Save The American Economy*

1 - Why I am Writing This Book

I talked previously about the need for a reason for prisoners to put out the effort needed to thrive. Every day is new and we can see the new possibilities that did not exist the previous day.

We will only have so many risings of the sun and none of us will ever know how many there are for us. We need each day to count towards the progress that we choose.

I Hope You Read

Prison Possibilities Family Time
A Reason to Thrive!

It Started the Conversation with:

Patience is A Virtue
Families Do Not Adapt Automatically
Spouses Do Not Adapt Easily Either
Communication & Continuation Of Love
PPDS Message Codes?
Harder for Mothers?
The Loss of a Father Connection
What About Calls and Visits?
Mindset Evaluation
Attitude Is Everything When Working with People"
Spousal Visits
The Importance of Time
Parent Child Time
Security of The Visit
Mini-Family Days
Time to Heal, Get Real & Deal
Children and Parents Stays

Blessed Is the Power Of Family Time
To Heal and Unify
All Members at All Levels
Even When It Seems Not to Be.

2 - Conflicting Priorities

Prison is rather intense and there are a lot of prisoners in a lot of prisons throughout the country. The prisoners are serving time and prison employees are doing their job.

Prisoners do not have the freedom that other citizens do so there is little opportunity for stresses to disperse naturally. Without release stress and tension can build up over time and predispose prisoners to be difficult to be with, work with or secure.

The rules of each facility are declared as a standard of behavior. Adherence to the rules can make everything easier for everybody.

Unfortunately, the priorities of various individuals may lead to behavior that does no coincide with the policies of administration. The major issue seems to be the security of the facility from many standpoints.

The rules are usually very facility specific and may apply to the coming and going of people within the facility and all that is allowed and prohibited within the walls.

Prison staff has the rules to enforce and that can be a challenge when there is a lack of cooperation. Employees must adhere to the requirements of their position and so they must enforce the rules.

3 - Security & Humanity

The prisons are challenged with the responsibility to provide security at every level of their operations. A balance is needed for all so that the individuality of everybody is respected as the great challenge of security is maintained.

Prisons are busy places and freedom of interaction is restricted so the kind of peace that free citizens might get to balance is not available to the incarcerated. So just being in prison has a consistent awareness of constriction and the absence of freedom.

The topic for this book is very pivotal to every aspect of the humanity of each prisoner. Security and humanity may be like water and oil where there is a natural tendency for separation.

It will take some work to promote the evolution of the concept that will help understanding that the tendency can be reversed for the benefit of all. While this will not be easy, it is important that clarity surfaces in all aspects of the discussion.

For me, the goal is to develop concepts enough so that the benefits come full circle to all willing participants. When you can help enough other people to get what they want, you will be able get what you want.

The sticking point in negotiations is usually to get the other party to set their limits first so the discussion can have a starting parameter. In this situation, there will not be a loser as long at the conversation continues. I invite all readers to make their preliminary list of their needs and wants to start the talk.

4 - Disclaimer

I, the author, am not involved with prisons or prisoners but I have talked to many during Hospital Pastoral Visitations. I am sharing what is coming to me in an effort to spread understanding and trigger conversation that can be helpful. It may be that the discussion needs finessing and I invite your wisdom in the mix.

My guidance has suggested that a lot can be done. I will detail my views which are not the expert positions of a Corrections Officer or Corrections Administrator or Corrections Manager or Corrections Supervisor, or Medical Practitioner or Psychologist or Psychiatrist or Social Worker or expert who might be helpful here.

As I have said many times before, everything that I look at about prisons seems to be so complicated. Here I suggest there may be many simple steps to consider.

I have written five books titled Prison Possibilities Dialogue Series and I invite submissions in the format specified. The core message about the series can be found for free at http://angelraphaelspeaks.com/prison-possibilities/ You will find twelve pages under the "Prison Possibilities" tab which give six sample dialogues.

Dialogues you want to share with me can be sent to ReverendMikeWanner@aol.com. I also encourage to publish in your area media.

5 - Let's Continue to Talk Family

The life of each prisoner started long before they went to jail and everybody has a different story so it is important that what went wrong is known to each person who is willing to participate. Things happen in families and sometimes problems are caused when things seemed to be a certain way that may have been different than what seemed to be.

To prepare for the future let us go back and look to heal wounds that are still open in the mind and experience. While history cannot be changed by looking back, we can sometimes revisit understanding and recalculate the intentions, process regrets and ready ourselves for healing.

Letting out the pain of the past can help allow healing. Understanding where others were in their heads at the time of events can also allow both healing and understanding.

Frequently, we may think that we know why people did what they did and then learn years later that their reasoning was not as we thought. It is common to think that we got hurt because someone was out to get us when they were really overwhelmed themselves and scared for their reasons.

Whatever you learn when you look back, the courage to go there will help you build character and confidence in your ability to stand up for yourself and move in to the future.

6 - The Human Need for Adjustment

When we buy a new pair of shoes, we are aware when our feet hurt and we have pain. A simple answer is usually to set aside those shoes for a little while and wear old shoes or slippers until the pain stops.

Later we will try again and see if we can stretch the time that we can tolerate the shoes until they start to hurt and give us pain. After a number of tries, the hurt and pain will disappear when we have adjusted to the shoes and/or the shoes have adjusted to our feet.

Feet are only one small part of the human experience. We can understand the need to adjust to them much better than we can our need to adjust to many things over our lives.

Feelings can be intense and run deep and things that happen to us can last for a long time because we do not always own the reality that we have experienced.

Recidivism for ex-prisoners can be very high and there are many theories on why. The theories seem to make some sense and offer solutions that seem logical but the theories do not seem to be grabbed up and implemented.

Why might you think that there is not an instantaneous change of circumstances after a story is written? I think that the story is a bandage over an untreated cause.

The problem will not go away until the cause is treated adequately. Stories can be diagnostic and point to a problem but that will not change the reality. If, however, the story is read by the right authority who can initiate change then, Change can manifest.

I am a veteran and have written veterans books and three specifically about PTSD. Post Trauma Stress Disorder is a condition where events create a disorder that survives the event and stresses the one who experienced the trauma.

Prisoners seem to have a level of Dissociation which is a component of PTSD and that explains to me many of the why's for the high level of recidivism. This may manifest as a tendency towards isolation and withholding of feelings which can be exacerbated by the prison lifestyle.

The absence of a safety zone of trust could cause an energy state that prisoners may use as a tool to cope with the absence of normal human interaction. The safety zone of which I speak is called family.

In my opinion, the lack of family and friends is devastating to the quality of life of prisoners and their ability to adjust later. This is not a diagnosis but it is my opinion.

The rest of this book will be about making baby steps to improve family bonding and prisoner support. Just like we need time to adjust to new shoes, adjusting to family healing prerelease may be a huge step forward in getting discharged prisoners to be ready when they leave so they can get out and stay out.

Blessed Is the Power of Family Time
To Heal and Unify

7 - Reconnecting with Family

Family could be easy or a real big challenge for prisoners. Family configurations vary greatly,

There are different levels of influence within families and it is important to identify the most influential members for each particular prisoner. I will probably write a separate book for prisoners to help them sort through the family dynamics that influence them most.

For the purpose of this book, I would like to convince the facilities to look at all they can do to help arrange available resources in a way that they can optimize communication time between prisoners and family. While I do not expect that there will be a sudden windfall of resources dropped from the sky, I would invite the utilization of all that they have available to maximize communication time.

The ideas that I would like to see developed might look like:
- PPDS Message Codes (As mentioned above)
- More Calls, Visits & Connectivity
- Mindset Evaluation
- Video Visitation via YouTube
- Spousal Visits in allowable formats
- Parent Child Time
- Security of The Visit
- Mini-Family Days
- Time to Heal, Get Real & Deal
- Child and Parents Time

8 - Ongoing Connectivity

A major point with human interaction is the consistency and frequency and expectancy. When someone has a connection with those they care about coming up, their days in advance can be much easier to live.

Ongoing connectivity can be accomplished in many ways. I invite prisoners and prison staff alike to begin to think of ways that they can contribute to a safe secure plan where prisoners can get more connectivity on a predictable basis.

Improving the comfort level of prisoner's connectivity can be very helpful to the peace in a facility. I would encourage making every effort to explore little steps that could be a big boost for prisoner's motivation.

With the high technology of systems on the outside, it could be relatively easy to receive and disburse e-mails to prisoners. Of course, that might raise some security concerns but I do believe that there could be a system developed that could respond in a formatted way that could tell those at home that the message was received.

If the book that I wrote on access controls was somewhat adopted then that pad may be a great way for prisoners to get their messages.

The institutional answers of years gone by are not satisfying to the prisoners of today. Yes, I do understand that a prisoner is not exactly a guest but in reality, dealing with people gets a lot easier when little gestures of courtesy are extended.

9 - Responses by Code

In the book - *Prison Possibilities Dialogue Series: Volume 4 Dialogues*, I proposed a rough outline of an idea to allow prisoners to send a coded message to their family that would be very simple and easily scanned for security.

The message codes were not completely thought out but I proposed some to start and that could be further developed. I suggest that as a starting point for a response system to be considered and built upon to something that could eventually be satisfactory to the administration of many facilities.

I have pasted that dialogue below for reference:

PPDS Message Codes?
[Dialogue 31]

Communication seems to be such a challenge for prisoners and their families so I wanted to float an idea about sending brief publicly available message codes to expedite a simple note.

A= all	A2= and	A3=as	A4= ARE
B= be	B2= best	B3= but	
C= can	C2= could		
D= do	D2= dear	D3=did	
E= I love my spouse			
F= for	F2=find		
G= good			
H= hi	H2=have	H3=how	
I=I	I2=if	I3=it	
J=just			

K=know
L= let   L2=location   L3=last
M= my   M2=maybe
N= no   N2=not   N3=need
O=ok
P= please   P2=page
Q=I love my child/children
R=rent   R2=re
S= so   S2=she
T= the   T2=thank   T3=thanks
U=you
V=very
W= we   W2=what   W3=when
X=thinking of you
Y=you   Y2=yes
$=money
!=important
@= a location
#=number
%=percentage
&=and

Examples:
"E Q H3 A4 U" = "I love my spouse, I love My Children. How are you"
"I N3 $" I need money"

Comments and code suggestions invited. Thanks.

10 - The Vulnerability to Prison Depression

The human condition is very sensitive to the emotions of time and place and people and music and many things. Health and wellness have roots in how one feels, what one feels they can do, what they are motivated to do and the freedom they have to do what they choose.

The harmonics of alignment can influence that which is reverberating in that space and any new reverberations added to that space. In music, you can hear when an instrument is not vibrating in balance with other instruments.

People can be in balance or out of balance in many circumstances. When people have their balancers, it can be relatively easy for them to move along in life.

I am pretty happy with the way things are in my life but when I started connecting with the energy of prisons, I was experiencing an uneasy state of mind. Even though I was invited by the Angels to make the connections, there was an ill at ease feeling of stress.

As soon as I would think about family, the stress would fade away quickly. Going back to the writing, the stress would return immediately.

Challenged was I, but not threatened. I knew the trigger and I knew the antidote.

I could proceed quite nicely by Angel connecting or family thought whenever I needed to break an uneasy link.

Prisoners may not be as empowered as I am since they are not in control of their circumstances and/or may not be as aware of the mental tools that I use. Patterns of thinking can be very effective at controlling feelings when a person is aware that they can take charge.

More often than not, people may have a tendency to feel limited by circumstance and accept the reality they see. Prison would not be the first choice of a location to choose for upliftment.

In the outside world, family space can be like a place of safety where creativity can flow without effort. Prison has the opposite effect.

When someone comes to prison because they made some mistakes and are mandated in to a new lifestyle that is more difficult than what they were familiar with, life can be downright hard. Without family in a place with a negative vibration, one will not be as able to feel safe and reclaim their powers or personal empowerment.

The daily cycles will not likely get easier until something positive happens but in prison that can take a long time. Prisoners are not necessarily the most friendly and gregarious people on the planet.

Without the safety of family connectivity, depression and vulnerability may hit new levels of trouble for prisoners. Depression of prisoners can spread like a virus since there are many stories that indicate mental illness is not unusual in prison.

11 - Power of Ramping Up Connectivity

Wherever your facility is on connectivity, I would encourage an effort to progressively increase the connections. The important parts are the progression, the frequency, the intensity and the expectancy or anticipation of the next connectivity time.

The idea is to increase connectivity in able to increase the motivation for the effort to thrive. People coming together can increase the energy that flows between them and provide a reason for the motivation to thrive.

Prisoners and prison staff can be influential in getting connectivity increased. To figure out how to do this, you will need to know the rules that apply at the facility.

It is impossible for anyone to know all the rules and regulations about correspondence at all the different facilities. Family connectivity is both a huge issue in ability to motivate but also it seems to be a big security issue for the facilities.

These conflicting priorities can cause a situation where everybody loses. Effort is needed to address the concerns and formulate issue sensitive remedies to the existing processes so that a whole new set of agreements is created to change the standard operating procedures on a fully integrated basis.

The engagement of prisoner contributors can be essential to the comprehensiveness of the effort. Trust is a key component to success and it can create many more options to the effectiveness and safety of facilities.

12 - Respected Prisoners

If there are prisoners who reach a level of respect and trust, they might just be candidates for rewards that can be helpful to the system and themselves.

Real rehabilitation does not happen by decree but it can emerge as developments can be justified by performance. Of course, it will be very challenging to the skills of corrections officers to balance trust, security and rehabilitation.

Small steps in the right direction may be fruitful and help ease tensions. Ongoing connectivity could be just the right reward because there is no cost to the facility but there can be huge perceived value for the prisoner to cooperate.

It can also make a huge difference in the possibilities for the future. To be successful as a facility, a decrease in recidivism could be an attention getter for the powers to be.

Prisoners starved for information may be seen as in better control but I wonder about that. Could it be that the opposite is true and that the lesser connected prisoners are a greater risk to the safety of everyone in the institution.

It seems to me that withholding social interaction from those who are already isolated is an explosion that is ready to happen.

There could be prisoners within the system who could receive coded replies from the prisoners and deliver them to a sending system to go back to families. If they ball gets dropped there is not harm just a bit less connectivity like now.

13 - Extended Family Can Help Also

Even if the immediate Spouse and children are unavailable to do visitations, the extended family could fill the void and provide more connectivity for the prisoners. r mf

The foundation early on for the prisoner was the family of yesteryear as he or she was growing up. The experience of those days past may have left impressions that could have been detrimental in the past or may, if healed now, be the foundation for the future.

If the prisoner has the chance for them to visit and talk, there could surface any unfinished issues that may have needed to be addressed but were not. While it may seem out of order for prisoners to go there before current family, many times the old stuff has influence over more recent circumstances.

There is an added benefit of talking to adults in that reconnection without children present can provide a platform for healing that would never to gotten to if the busyness of younger folks was present.

If it is possible to provide quiet uncongested space with no one listening then a lot more could be accomplished in a lot less time. After a prisoner is unaccustomed to the safety of family for a long time, it may take a bit until the guardedness settles.

Apologies may need to be spoken. Regrets may be shared and that can happen lot easier if there is private time.

It will take time for all to learn that they are not the only one in a family who felt unfilled by family interaction. Time does help but it is not a universal remedy. Sometimes, expressing an apology or a regret can be much better received than one might expect.

It is not wise to expect too much too soon or to expect that everyone will welcome the prisoner back with open arms. Healing takes time.

Caution is suggested so that prisoners take reasonable efforts to make nice but resist being abused in the process, especially by your siblings. Parents also could be a challenge that needs more patience.

Confidence and consideration can go a long way to optimizing the connections.

14 - Types of Connectivity

Every bit of time that a prisoner can spend in positive time is a whole lot better than spending the same time in a negative state of mind.

I have never been convicted of anything but a speeding ticket but I have been separated from family while I was in the United States Air Force. The days were long and the clock ticked ever so slowly but I knew the length of my stay.

Time away from family is hard but prison is in a way like the military as you never know exactly what is going to happen. There are unpredictable people and events that can happen at any time and change the quality of your day.

The military may even be easier than prison because in the service, there are people who depend on you for their own security. They want you to survive so that they are not without the same level of support that they started the day with.

In the military, every letter or contact mattered and I suspect it is the same for most prisoners.

When you are feeling disconnected, everything can be a struggle. I invite everybody reading this to put of their thinking caps and plan, design and arrange circumstances which can bring reasonable options for those who are incarcerated.

Nobody expect a prisoner to have as much communication as a free person but that should not stop any of us from pushing the ideas forward that can promote connectivity.

Everything can make a difference. A tweet could be like gold to someone who is desperate.

A greeting card could change many possibilities and keep someone from acting out and hurting people. Pressure cookers have pressure relief valves. Prisons do not seem to.

Types of things that might help:
1. Coded messages like above.
2. Tweets that get delivered.
3. Greeting Cards either real or electronic.
4. Telephone visits.
5. Video visits.
6. Private Audio time.
7. Visitations of all kinds.
8. A safe cell where prisoners could get a break from Their paranoia episodes.
9. Choices options for association or friendship circles.
10. Special interest groups.
11. Parent Child Time
12. Spousal Visits.
13. Special benefits as rewards for special efforts.

The whole issue of Connectivity is about Dignity and respect for the humanity of the individual.

15 - Safety Discussions

Prisons safety meetings could be a huge issue for prisoners to vent some of their feelings of vulnerability. They can also be a major opportunity for corrections staff to learn about potential weaknesses in the internal security system.

Small groups of perhaps six could be comingled from different sections of the facility and provide fresh faces that stimulate feelings of safety for attendees.

Readers may feel that I am off topic and I am a bit but the internal connectedness can build upon the benefits from family. When a prisoner gets out, they will need to interact with others outside the family and prison is a good place to practice reconnecting with people outside the family again.

The stories available to the general public talk about the vulnerability in great detail because it is difficult for prisoners to open up and that may have a big influence on discharge's ability to reconnect.

The goals of prisons could include helpful components to help prisoners get out and stay out. The more that can be done in prison and with family to help the prisoners bridge the crevice that need to get past will do a lot.

Veterans and prisoners and others who have felt vulnerable can carry that vulnerability for a long time and it can impede their return to the "Normal" world. Let's start early and work hard to get people ready to leave prison forever.

16 - Security During Visit

Length of the visit could be paramount to success so we need to talk about security and planning to do increased time for prisoners who are likely to be recoverable. If one goes through security screening at the airport for a flight, the security time for screening may be the same for a hour long flight as for an international flight of much longer duration.

Once inside the security zone, cleared passengers are allowed to traverse the space at their will. This offers a tremendously Beneficial dynamic to the time that they spend at the airport and allow them to pleasantly pass the time that they are waiting.

Security at prisons may not be as hospitable and one has to wonder what could be done to increase the peacefulness of the visits for those who are family members of the prisoners. We all know that security is important but we also know that people under stress can pose threats that would ordinarily be non-existent.

I would encourage consideration of much longer stays than the ones normal at prisons. Additional diligence for a longer visit could be very worthwhile to visitors and prisoners at reaching deeper understanding, comprehension and bonding.

The quality of the visit could be enhanced by total absolute privacy of conversation but a video monitor could be allowed. Suggest that the prisoner and visitor know that their conversation is unmonitored unless an alert sounds that the mute is off. Visit time minimum stay suggestion is 3 hours.

17 - Little Steps to A Solid Foundation

The baby steps above are the beginning steps on a path to building a stronger foundation for prisoners. Those who are denied extended connectivity should be the ones who have behaved in a way that makes them less worthy of consideration.

I do not know how to define less worthy, but it may be easy for correctional staff who see the behavior on a daily basis.

Family connectivity can be rebuilt but it may take much more time than is allowed by visitation policies. I cannot imagine how much time prisoners may need to get ready to reconnect with their families.

Time is needed to reconnect and it is my suggestion that the earlier the process starts, the better might be the results. While I am not a practitioner of psychological treatment, I have talked to many people in distress and there always seems to be connected to times or events that are not obviously connected.

A helpful process may also be to find prisoners who are credentialed or experienced in the listening arts so that a safe environment can be found for more healing prior to release.

Emotional healing can help prisons to be safer for all. Of course, efforts must be diligent and appropriate.

Safe talking areas could be promoted in the general population to help bring down stress and promote community.

18 - Stay Value Extenders

The value of reconnection efforts is in progression and repetition. The extended visits of three hours or more can amplify results.

The main idea is to avoid intermittent interaction scarcity and increase connectivity. Ongoing connectivity allows the memories to stay warm and vibrant and supportive.

Ideas to also consider may be Google, Facebook, any social media program and community events programs.

Separately, I have written about Prison Possibilities Access Systems with the suggestion included of having separate prisoner tracking and prison shift programs that may be made possible by access control systems that could create flow patterns with facilities that would adapt and incorporate them.

The shifts discussed in that separate book could allow anybody participating in a shift to access permitted areas by requests approved by corrections officers or by programmed authorization of persons permitted to interact.

19 - Time to Heal, Get Real & Deal

The success of extended connectivity for prisoners is not just about the prison peace for the prisoner. It is about the total family and that brings the opportunity for the family to heal from the problems and issues of the past.

Healing while the prisoner is still in prison is much more desirable than waiting until they are discharged. When they get out, they will be faced with all the issues of day to day survival that they have not dealt with for a long time. Healing some things while still in prison may make the difference of whether one is ready to get out and stay out.

When someone gets cancer, the doctors like to attack it when it is small so they have the best chance of the patient surviving. The afflictions in one's negative life experiences are similar as it is better to solve the problems earlier than later.

Prisoners may have unresolved issues that are best resolved earlier rather than later. When you can fix old stuff before you get out, your stress will be less when out and your opportunities for success will be more and hopefully optimized.

Also, while you are still inside, you can help to lighten the load for everyone else inside and show that there is hope available for those who desire to work their way out of their history and pave a new future for themselves and others.

Hope makes the days pass with a peace that is not found in anxiety and despair. Peace is powerful and spreadable and can bring great joy to many.

20 - Children and Parents Days & Stays

We can expand on the day visits and create a series of stays where there is a level of accommodation created for families.

The more normal the time, the more benefit to the family. Vacation together and stay together for ever and ever Amen.

Staging and presentation would continue to send a message of possibility throughout the facility and encourage more joy. The Length of Stays could be steadily increased as it made sense to the whole community.

Life for prisoners has been cast in a pattern of older ideas. Let's take some time to plan new possibilities for the nation that allows efficiency and kindness.

The hope is that resources can be reallocated to provide a better utilization that is congruent with new options for all those who live in our cities. Education could get a boost from more resources.

Care programs could expand as could treatment programs and Early Childhood Education. Options can improve the quality of life for many.

Children Are Our Future.
Healing Can Help Families.
Parents At Home Can Help Healing.

For
Considering
These
Ideas

Ever

It Does Not Help Prayer Still Does!

Resource http://www.Create-A-Prayer.com

23 - Resource List

Distant Healing Sessions (or Join Mail List) – Write To mikewann@voicenet.com

Books by Rev. Mike at www.Amazon.com

Veterans Healing Six Pack
1. *Trauma Healing Options for VA Hospitals: Help for Veterans to Own Their Healing and their future.*
2. *Trauma Healing Action Steps for Veterans: Help to Start Healing*
3. *Trauma Healing Action Steps for Veterans: Empowerment*
4. *Trauma Healing Action Steps for Veterans: Forgiveness*
5. *Trauma Healing Action Steps for Veterans: Thought Freedom*
6. *Tea For Veterans: Welcome One Home*

PTSD Power Pack:
1. *The PTSD Project: Turn Pain To Power*
2. *PTSD & Soul Retrieval: Putting One Back Together*
3. *PTSD & The Purple PAD: Calling all Scientists and PTSD Patients*

Angel Raphael Speaks Volume 1: Take Courage! God Has Healing in Store for You!
Angel Raphael Speaks Volume 2: Take Courage! God Has Healing in Store for You!
Angel Raphael Speaks Volume 3: Take Courage! God Has Healing in Store for You!
Angel Raphael Speaks Volume 4: Angels, Addicts, Alcoholics & Prisoners – Oh Yeah!
Angel Raphael Speaks Volume 5: Prisoners Caring for Alcoholics - Australia In Miniature Projects Intro
Angel Raphael Speaks Volume 6: Prisoners Caring for Addicts - Australia In Miniature For Addicts
Reiki Journaling from Japan
Reiki Is Alive: God's Great Gift
Four Parts to Healing
Distant Healing: We Are All Connected
Stress Release Energy Work: How To Cope
Does Reiki Love Heal Cancer?
Group Consciousness

Salute To Philadelphia VA Medical Center: Thank You
Reiki Transcript for Reiki 2 & 3 Channels: Dr. Usui Is That You?
God Bless Kindle & Amazon
Puppies Are Different From People
If Your Dog Dies
Toy Guns Are Obsolete
Great Spirit Made Children With Red Skin: AND
The Cage of Fear: Is Not Locked
God Made Children Red, Yellow, Brown, Black & White: Greet Each Child With Kindness
Emergency Medical Kindness In The Cradle Of Liberty: Big City - Cracked Bell
Angels Are Always Around Addicts and Addicts: Help Is Near Now! Invite It In!
Angels Are Always Around Addicts and Alcoholics: Volume 2 - Tools To Help Re-Light Your Life
Prison Jobs Now: Providing Care For Addicts And Addicts
Controlled Care Communities Concept
Prison Possibilities Dialogue Series: Concept
Prison Possibilities Dialogue Series: Volume 2, 3, 4, 5 Dialogues
Prison Possibilities Voluntary Exile
Prison Possibilities Corrections Coaches
Prison Possibilities For Mexicans: Is A Boat Better Than A Wall?
Prison Possibilities Family Time: A Reason to Thrive!
Prison Genius Pool: "So Much Genius In Jail"

Little Books at Kindle.com by Rev. Mike:
English Medical History Questionnaire For Non-English Speakers
English Language Helper For Non-English Speakers
Wise Wonderful Women Are The Well Of The Family
Answers for Test & Research: Dowsing Power
Crisis? Reiki! Baby? Reiki!
Bible References For Healing
Angel Raphael Speaks – Prisons
Angel Raphael Speaks – Veterans
The Saint Off Interstate 95

Angel Raphael Speaks through Rev. Mike Wanner. Please visit
http://www.AngelRaphaelSpeaks.com

24 - Angels Please Prayers

Addict's
Angels of Healing Selected
Help Me to Stay Directed
Come To Me From The Sky
I Am Ready to Succeed Not Try
If I Don't Invite You In
I Might Not Win
I Have Been Lost For Too Long
Help Me To Stay Strong

Alcoholic's
Angels of Healing On High
Help Me to Stay Dry
Come To Me From The Sky
I Am Ready to Succeed Not Try
If I Don't Invite You In
I Might Not Win
I Have Been Lost For Too Long
Help Me To Stay Strong

From

http://AngelRaphaelSpeaks.com/AAAAAAA/

25 - Private Channeling

Angel Raphael Speaks is a series of free messages that are channeled through Reverend Mike Wanner for the Highest good and Highest Healing of all concerned.

Many questions arise about Reverend Mike doing private channeling and he does help with that so e-mail him.

Reverend Mike is available world-wide as a psychic channel, emotional release facilitator, spiritual energy practitioner & teacher, and public speaker. He looks forward to meeting you soon!

Email - mikewann@voicenet.com 215-342-1270 PRIVATE SPIRITUAL READINGS/channelings or Spiritual Healing Sessions: Telephone or in person. Rev. Mike is available for private, one-on-one intuitive sessions with you, his Guide Family, and your Guides. He helps by offering clarity on emotional situations about your life, your purpose, your spirituality, and the release of stuffed emotions and cellular memory.

Connect to the love of your Guides today!

Contact Rev. Mike for an appointment.

Sessions available:

Spiritual Readings
Angel Channeling
Distant Reiki Healing
Distant Clearing of Stuffed Emotions
Distant Clearing Cellular Memory
Distant Clearing Energy Blockages
Distant Clearing of the Chakras
Customized needs
Mastermind dowsing responses to yes/no direction finding questions.

Rev. Mike is a facilitator of healing. He brings you and the Divine together so that you can align with the Divine and have a great time and a great life. All healing is between you and God, as it should be. Go ahead and start without Rev. Mike. Visit his prayer site http://www.Create-A-Prayer.com. Take the first step NOW.

26 - Reverend Mike Wanner

Rev. Mike Wanner started his metaphysical and ministerial studies with Reiki in 1993 and has studied seven styles of Reiki in the U.S., Japan, Canada, Denmark and Australia. He is certified to teach. He became certified to teach Integrated Energy Therapy in 1999 and co-taught the first IET class of the new Millennium. Mike began dowsing in 2001.

Ordained as a Metaphysical Minister of the International Metaphysical Ministry and an Interfaith Minister of the Circle of Miracles Ministry, Rev. Mike practices and teaches spiritual energy therapies in the Philadelphia Area.

Rev. Mike holds ministerial degrees from the University of Metaphysics and the University of Sedona. He is a Pastoral Care Associate of Aria - Frankford Hospital. He taught at the National Academy of Massage Therapy and Health Sciences.

Rev. Mike was a faculty member of the Medical Mission Sister's Center for Human Integration's School of Integrated Body/Mind Therapies in Fox Chase, Philadelphia, PA for twelve years.

Rev. Mike is licensed by the teaching of Intuitional Metaphysics to practice Spiritual Healing and Scientific Prayer. Mike is also a Prayer therapist.

Rev. Mike was elected in 2007 to the status of "Fellow of the American Institute of Stress."

In 2008, Rev. Mike became a practitioner of Coincidental Recognition as he incorporated the CoRe System in to his spiritual healing practice.

In 2009, Rev. Mike trademarked a new healing process called Quantum Quatro! Subtle Energy System Support®.

In 2011, Rev. Mike joined the outreach program known as the Health Advantage Group.

In 2012, Rev. Mike became a Certified Professional Coach by The Master Coaching Academy and Joined the Personal Empowerment Group.

Prior to his metaphysical, ministerial and coaching studies, Rev. Mike worked for Sears Roebuck and Co. while in High School and after graduation until he joined the U. S. Air Force in 1965. He returned to Sears from Vietnam in 1969 and stayed until 1978. His final Sears assignment was as an efficiency expert in Methods - Operational Research and Development.

He volunteered with Burholme Emergency Medical Services from 1969 and is still a Life Member and Board of Directors Member. He started a private ambulance company in 1975 and worked professionally in the field until 2001 when he devoted his full attention to real estate investing, healing, coaching and writing.

www.ReverendMikeWanner.com

www.ingramcontent.com/pod-product-compliance
Lightning Source LLC
Chambersburg PA
CBHW061234180526
45170CB00003B/1287